THE JOURNEY OF TUNURI AND THE BLUE DEER

A HUICHOL INDIAN STORY

JAMES ENDREDY

ILLUSTRATED BY
MARÍA HERNÁNDEZ DE LA CRUZ
AND CASIMIRO DE LA CRUZ LÓPEZ

Bear Cub Books
Rochester, Vermont

Bear Cub Books
One Park Street
Rochester, Vermont 05767
www.InnerTraditions.com

Bear Cub Books is a division of Inner Traditions International

Library of Congress Cataloging-in-Publication Data

Endredy, James.
  The journey of Tunuri and the Blue Deer : a Huichol Indian story / James Endredy ; illustrated by María Hernández de la Cruz and Casimiro de la Cruz López.
      p. cm.
Summary: Retells a traditional Huichol tale in which the young Tunuri learns his place in the natural world when, after being lost in the forest, he meets the magical Blue Deer and follows him on a special journey.
  ISBN 1-59143-016-X
  1. Huichol Indians—Folklore. 2. Tales—Mexico. [1. Huichol Indians—Folklore. 2. Indians of Mexico—Folklore. 3. Folklore—Mexico.] I. Hernández de la Cruz, María, ill. II. Cruz López, Casimiro de la, ill. III. Title.

F1221.H9E63 2003
398.2'089'9745—dc21

2003052298

Printed and bound in China

10 9 8 7 6 5 4 3 2 1

Text design and layout by Mary Anne Hurhula
This book was typeset in Bulmer with Ashley Crawford as the display typeface

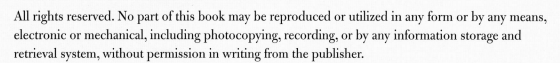

Acknowledgments

From the moment of its birth, this book has been a gift to me from my main spiritual teachers: Earth, Water, Wind, Sun, Fire, Deer, Trees, Birds, and Hikuri. To them I humbly offer my work.

I give grateful thanks to my Huichol elders, brothers, and sisters for allowing me a glimpse from the inside into their ancient and sacred Earth-honoring tradition.

Very special thanks to Elaine Sanborn for giving life to this project, and to the whole Inner Traditions • Bear & Company crew, especially to Ehud Sperling, Jon Graham, Rob Meadows, Jeanie Levitan, and Jody Winters. It's an honor and privilege to work with people who put so much heart and soul into what they do.

Last, profound thanks without words to the sacred land of Wirikuta, which inspired this book.

One day the families of a village in the mountains of Mexico began walking through the woods on their way to the sacred mountain, which was far away in Wirikuta and took many days to reach. Along with the adults in one of the families was a small boy named Tunuri. Because he was very adventurous, Tunuri loved the long journey to the sacred mountain and often liked to walk where his parents couldn't see him.

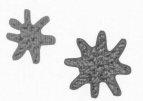

I n the middle of their journey, as they walked in the early morning light, Tunuri saw a beautiful butterfly with wings of many colors, and he decided to follow it to see where it was going. He ran with the butterfly over many hills and through the forest—until he looked around and realized that he couldn't hear or see anyone anymore.

There were no voices and there was no laughter in the air. The forest was full of shadows and stillness. He knew then that he was far away from his family—he was lost! Tunuri was afraid. He turned in every direction, trying to see something familiar, but he didn't know where he was or which way to go.

7

Then something caught his eye. What was it? Tunuri looked up and saw a family of deer standing at the top of the next hill, and one of the deer was walking toward him. As the animal came closer, Tunuri knew that this was no ordinary deer, for his coat was a lovely deep blue—and he glowed all over, as if the sun or moon shone from inside him.

As he came near, the magical Blue Deer spoke. "Hello, Tunuri. I know you are lost and I know where your family is. Grandfather Fire has sent me to show you where you can find them. You must follow me—and hurry, so they won't miss you!"

T hen the Blue Deer turned and ran away. Tunuri was disappointed. He wanted to follow the Blue Deer, but the animal moved too quickly. Tunuri looked at the ground, wanting to cry—and saw right away that wherever the Blue Deer had stepped, there were now colorful flowers growing! The footprints of the magical deer made a trail of beautiful flowers for him to follow.

9

Tunuri began to walk, following this flower trail. He walked up a high hill and standing in the sun at the very top was the Blue Deer. Tunuri ran up to him and saw the sun shining brightly in the sky. As he enjoyed its warmth on his skin, he heard a strong, kind voice speak. "Hello, Tunuri! I am Father Sun."

Tunuri was surprised and turned his face to the bright sky. "You and all other beings are my children," the voice said. "I am father to everything on Earth, and in my light and warmth and energy the trees grow tall, the flowers bloom, and the fruit ripens. My light shines from your eyes and lives in your heart. You can feel my warmth on your skin and see the beautiful colors I paint on the clouds. I am here for you, my son. Remember that you can talk to me whenever you wish."

Tunuri was filled with happiness from Father Sun's warmth and care. "Thank you, Father Sun! I will always remember."

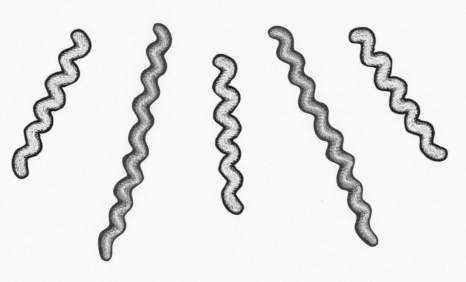

The Blue Deer then turned and ran away again, and as he ran, he called to Tunuri, "Follow me! Your family is waiting for you!" Tunuri followed the flowers again until he came to a beautiful wide valley between two great mountains. As he joined the Blue Deer he suddenly felt a wind blowing through the valley, cool and fresh. The leaves of the trees began to dance, the tall grasses swayed back and forth, and the birds above them flew effortlessly in the sky.

Tunuri then heard a singing voice, "Hello, Tunuri! I am Brother Wind. Because the Sun is my father too, you and I are brothers. In fact, I am the eldest brother of all beings, and I give the breath of life to all children. When I blow strongly, I move the sky, and when I blow gently, you can hear me whispering. I am here, Tunuri, whenever you need me. Just take a deep breath, and I am with you."

Tunuri breathed in deeply and felt the fresh wind fill his lungs. "Good to meet you, Brother Wind. I will breathe and visit with you!"

14

And with that, the Blue Deer ran again and called to Tunuri, "Follow me! We're going to visit your sister."

Soon they came to a shining lake. Tunuri stood next to the Blue Deer on the lake's shore and watched the many animals drinking there. Then he looked into the clear water and saw all kinds of fish swimming. On the surface of the lake he could see the reflection of the sky above. He bent down and took a small sip of the cool water, and just then the water spoke to him.

"Hello, Tunuri," the water said in a cool and lilting voice. "I am Sister Water. Wind is my brother and Sun is my father. I quench the thirst of all Earth's animals and plants. Whenever you stand in the rain or by a stream, a lake, or an ocean, I will be with you. Drink me and I will nourish your body. I will be your sister forever."

Tunuri splashed some of Sister Water's cool drops on his face. "Thank you, Sister Water. I will always remember you," he said happily.

Then the Blue Deer said, "Follow me, Tunuri. Your mother is waiting!"

Following the animal's colorful trail, Tunuri reached a magnificent garden full of fruit trees and flowers and vegetables. Birds sang in the trees, Father Sun shone brightly, Brother Wind blew gently, and Sister Water sent a soft rain. A colorful rainbow arched across the sky over the garden. It was the most beautiful place Tunuri had ever seen. He stood in amazement, and the Blue Deer said, "Put your hands on the ground, Tunuri, and feel where all this beauty grows from."

Tunuri walked beside the Blue Deer until they reached a large cave. Inside, standing in a circle around a large fire, were six more Blue Deer. Tunuri laughed with pleasure and excitement.

"These are my brothers and sisters," said the Blue Deer, "and we live here with Grandfather Fire. He has been waiting for you. In order to see him, take a small stick from the ground, say out loud all the things you have seen and felt today, and then place the stick in the fire and he will come to you."

Tunuri did this and placed a small twig in the flames. He watched as the flames moved upward and their sparks formed little stars. Then he heard a deep, old voice. "Welcome, Tunuri! I am Grandfather Fire. I live in all the stars in the sky. My children are Sun and Earth—and you are my grandson. I asked the Blue Deer to introduce you to your family—Father Sun, Mother Earth, Brother Wind, and Sister Water— because they love you. Now that you know them, you will never be alone again, even if you are lost."

"**B**ut I also asked the Blue Deer to bring you here so that I could give you a special task: I want you to share with your human family—and with all the people you know and meet—what you have learned today. Do you think you can do that, Tunuri?"

Tunuri was filled with the wonderful heat and strength of Grandfather Fire. "Yes, I can do it! I will share with everyone I know, and I will take them to visit all of you—Father Sun and Mother Earth, Brother Wind and Sister Water—so they can talk to you and know you just as I do."

"Very good, Tunuri," said Grandfather Fire, and the stars above him shone even more brightly. "Always remember that if you need me, you have only to look up to the stars in the night sky."

"Thank you, Grandfather," said Tunuri. "I will remember."

"It is time now for you to go back to your human family and begin your task, Tunuri," said the Blue Deer. "When you leave this cave, follow my footprints. They will lead you in the right direction. Good-bye, my friend! Maybe we will meet again someday."

"Good-bye," said Tunuri. Then he quickly kissed the soft, glowing cheek of the Blue Deer and turned to follow the trail of flowers.

When Tunuri reached his family, they were overjoyed to find him well and safe. He was very happy to be with his mother and father again and told them all about the Blue Deer and the important task that Grandfather Fire had given him.

As he lay down to sleep that night, Tunuri could see Grandfather Fire twinkling in all the stars in the dark sky. He felt the embrace of Mother Earth beneath him and the cool breath of Brother Wind as he blew through the trees. Sister Water sang him a soft lullaby in the stream nearby.

"Good night, Tunuri," they all whispered to him as he fell asleep. "If you remember us and the task that Grandfather Fire has given you, every day will be as magical as this day has been."

"Good night," whispered Tunuri, as he drifted off to sleep.

HUICHOL SACRED SYMBOLS

The drawings in *The Journey of Tunuri and the Blue Deer* are filled with creatures and objects that are sacred symbols to the Huichol people. Each of them represents something very important, and many of them are used in Huichol sacred practices and offerings. See how many of these you can find in the story's drawings.

This is a *muvieri,* the shaman's (priest's) wand that helps him communicate with the world of nature and spirit. It is made from Brazil wood and sacred eagle feathers.

This is a *prayer arrow,* which is used as a sacred offering to the spirits by men and boys. It is made from Brazil wood and reed and is painted with colored resin.

This is the *rirriki,* the sacred house and temple where prayer offerings are kept.

This is a *nierika,* a portal between our world and the spirit world.

This is the *sacred butterfly,* who announces the arrival of transformative visions.

This is *Kahullumari, the spirit deer,* who is the guide, messenger, and guardian of the sacred desert of Wirikuta.

This is the *sacred eagle,* messenger of Father Sun and the sacred places.

These are the *sacred snakes,* spirit animals of the rain.

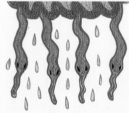

This is *hikuri,* the sacred peyote cactus that lives in the desert of Wirikuta.

These are a *prayer gourd and candle,* which are used as sacred offerings by women and girls. The inside of the gourd is covered with beeswax and is then beautifully adorned with colored beads or yarn.

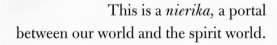

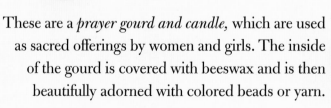

WHO ARE THE HUICHOL?

The Huichol Indians are among the last of the world's indigenous cultures that have been able to maintain their way of life and spiritual traditions into this new millennium. They live in remote regions of the Sierra Madre Mountains of western Mexico. Although some of their villages that lie near Mexican towns can now be reached by car, many of their communities and ceremonial centers are still isolated by mountainous terrain.

Nature is truly the home of the Huichol. Without supermarkets for food, electricity for lights or television, and roads for transportation, they practice sustenance farming, walk wherever they go, and wake and sleep with the cycles of the sun and moon. Their rich, nature-based spiritual tradition permeates every aspect of their life. For them, everything in the environment is alive, containing life force or soul. This is why corn, clouds, trees, flowers, and even rocks are sacred.

Most sacred of all are the spirits that give life to and nourish the world: Sun, Earth, Water, Air and Fire. The Huichol express their reverence for these natural powers in terms of kinship, calling them, as Tunuri learns to call them, our "Father Sun" or our "Mother Earth." Another important spirit is the Blue Deer—Kahullumari—who is the messenger between the worlds of mortals and spirits.

The Journey of Tunuri and the Blue Deer is a modern adaptation of a traditional Huichol story of a boy or girl finding his or her task in life by connecting with the powers of nature through the help of the sacred Blue Deer and the sacred cactus, *hikuri,* two of the most important elements of the Huichol spiritual tradition. It is important to note that this story is not based on a legend or fable; on the contrary, all of its characters (except Tunuri and his family) and places are as real to the Huichol as our families and homes are to us.

The setting of the story is Wirikuta, a special area in the state of St. Louis Potosi, Mexico, to which the Huichol make pilgrimages to find a "vision" that guides their life. It is here in Wirikuta that they encounter Kahullumari, from whose footprints grow the sacred flowers of *hikuri* (peyote). Through the visions delivered by Kahullumari and hikuri, the pilgrims find answers to questions such as Who am I ?, Why am I here?, and What is my task in life?

The sacred mountain Ra´ Unarre, where Father Sun—Tayau—was born, is found in Wirikuta. The Huichol have many sacred sites, and in this story Kahullumari takes Tunuri to some of them so that he can meet his sacred relatives where they live. Tunuri visits Rapavillame, or Lake Chapala in Spanish; Tatai Urianaka—Mother Earth; and Tekata, where Grandfather Fire lives. The Huichol routinely make pilgrimages to these places as part of their annual ceremonial calendar. They bring offerings to the sacred sites in order to show respect and keep balance between their communities and the forces of Nature that give them life.

However, they don't do it for themselves alone. Like the Hopi of the southwestern United States, the Huichol believe that their sacred tradition of pilgrimages, offerings, and prayers keeps balance for the whole world and all living beings, and if they were to stop or be unable to continue such honoring, it would mean the end of the world. This is one reason why the elders and leaders of contemporary Huichol communities now spend much time and effort trying to maintain and preserve the sacred sites. Even so, many are in serious danger of destruction.

It is my hope that sharing stories such as *The Journey of Tunuri and the Blue Deer* will heighten awareness of the nature-based cultures that still survive on our marvelous planet. Despite all our differences in lifestyle, we all share the same Sun, Earth, Air, and Water, which means we are all connected in this sacred web of life.

To find out how you can help preserve Huichol sacred sites and culture, visit www.JamesEndredy.com.

How Each Yarn Drawing for this Book Was Made

All of the illustrations in this book are drawings made from yarn that is applied to a piece of wood. To create this unique art form, artists María and Casimiro first spread a thin layer of beeswax on a board with their fingers. For pictures that have symmetrical designs, such as Father Sun on page 12, Casimiro etches some perpendicular and parallel guidelines into the wax.

Using small scissors, Casimiro and María carefully press the yarn into the wax. First they define the border for the picture. Next, María creates the outlines for all the main figures.

After all the outlines are complete, Casimiro and María fill in these figures with many colors of yarn, and add all the details, such as flowers and tiny creatures and many sacred Huichol symbols. The background of the drawing—the sky and ground, and all the color around the figures—is the last element to be filled in.

Each drawing takes many hours to complete, requiring enormous amounts of patience, skill, and artistic vision. Huichols have long practiced this art—learning to make ever more complex and beautiful pictures with wood, wax, and yarn. María and Casimiro teach this special technique to younger members of the Huichol community to keep this artistic tradition alive.

Original Huichol yarn drawings are available for purchase. For information contact the author at www.JamesEndredy.com